BIG NOTE PIANO

Alfred

VERY MERRY CHRISTMAS SONGS

Arranged by DAN COATES

Dan COATES

D0746400

CONTENTS

DAN COATES® is a registered trademark of Alfred Publishing Co., Inc.

© 2004 ALFRED PUBLISHING CO., INC.
All Rights Reserved

DECK THE HALL

TRADITIONAL OLD WELSH
Arranged by DAN COATES

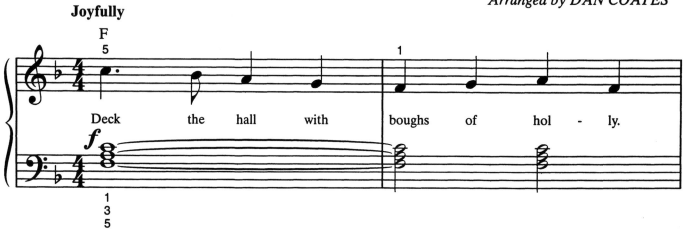

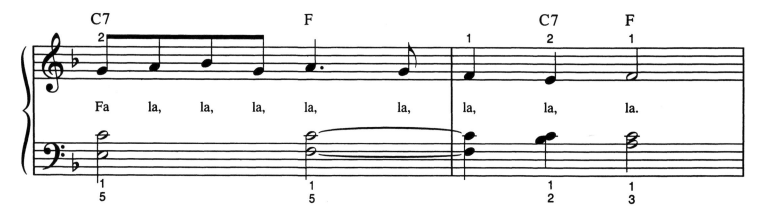

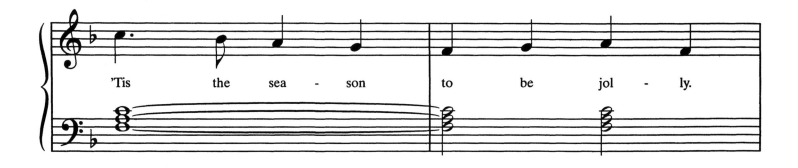

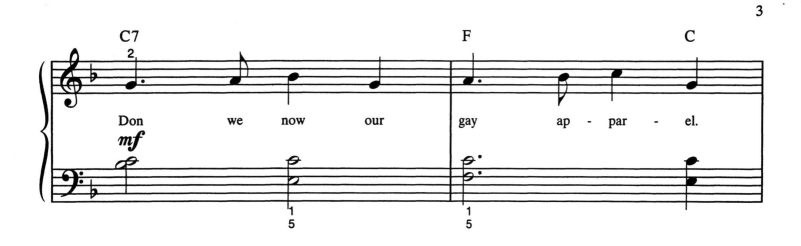

Don we now our gay ap - par - el.

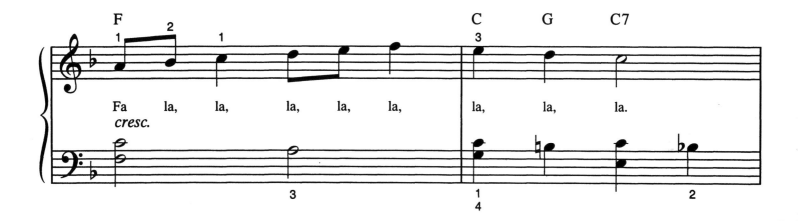

Fa la, la, la, la, la, la, la, la.

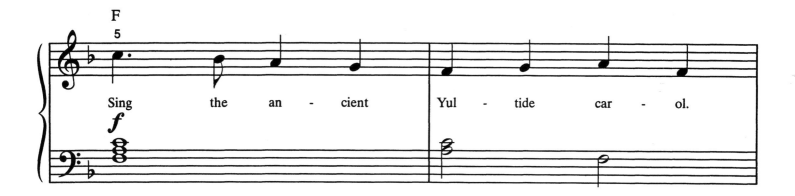

Sing the an - cient Yul - tide car - ol.

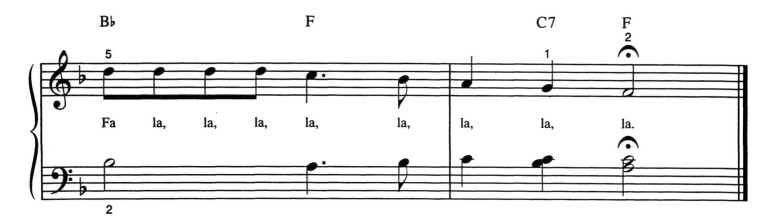

Fa la, la, la, la, la, la, la, la.

Deck the Hall - 2 - 2
AFM0406

FROSTY THE SNOWMAN

Music and Lyrics by
STEVE NELSON and JACK ROLLINS
Arranged by DAN COATES

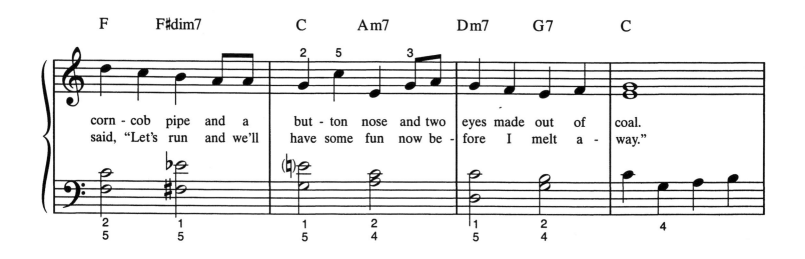

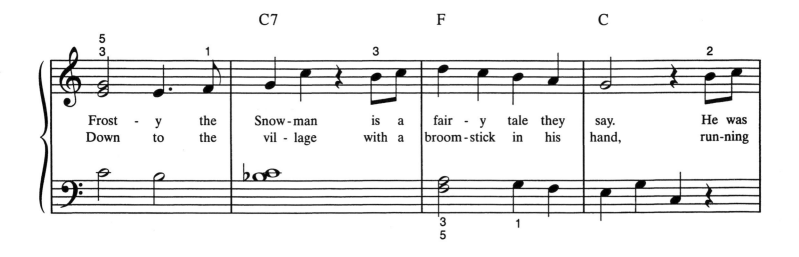

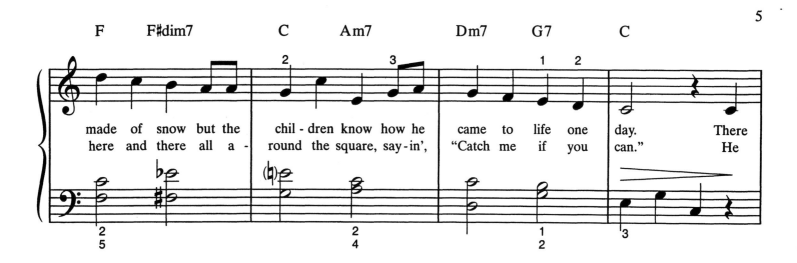

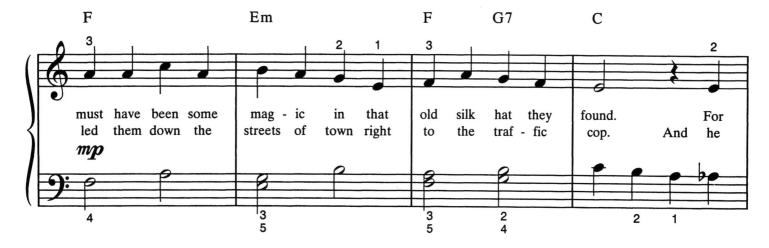

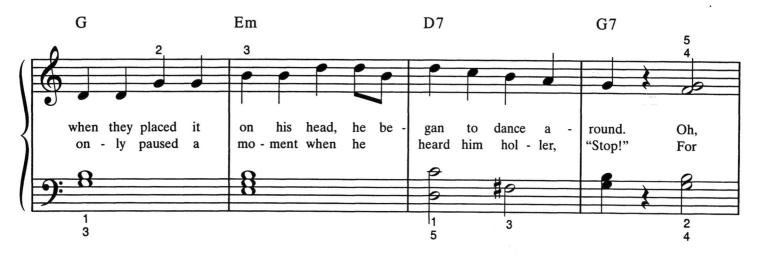

6

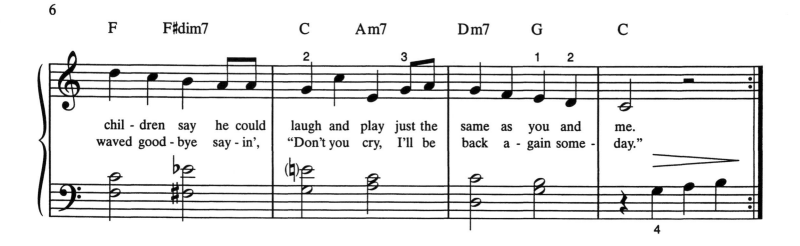

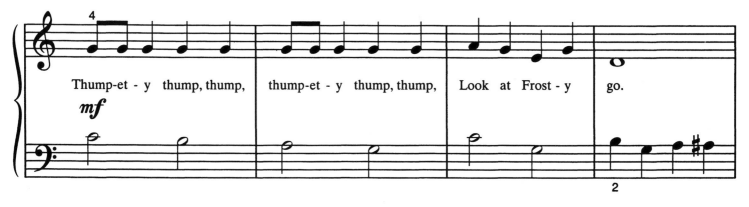

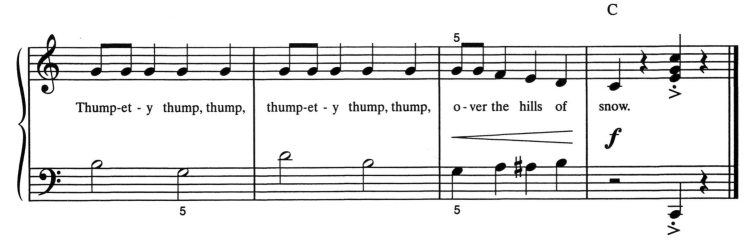

IT'S THE MOST WONDERFUL
TIME OF THE YEAR

By
EDDIE POLA and GEORGE WYLE
Arranged by DAN COATES

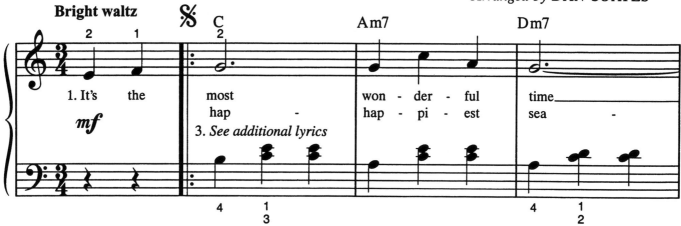

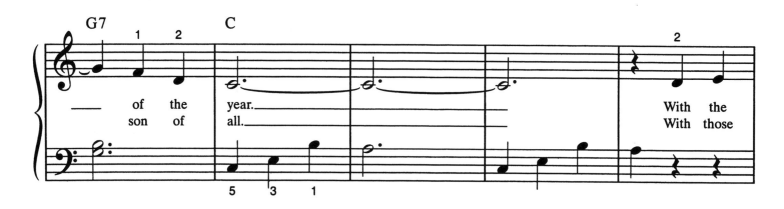

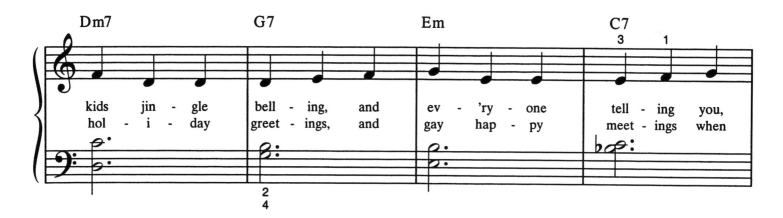

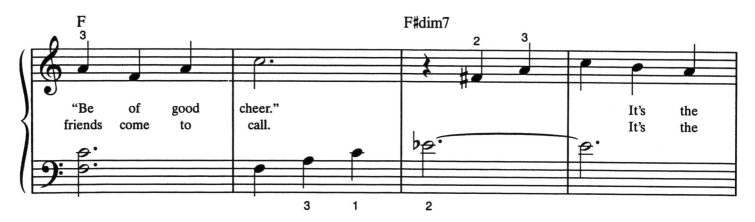

The Most Wonderful Time of Year - 3 - 1
AFM0406

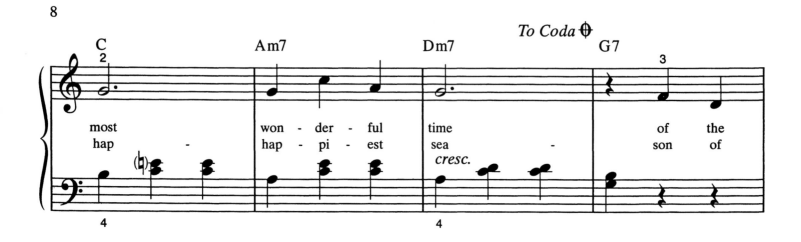

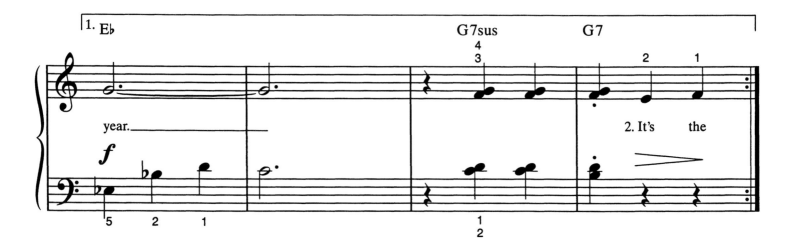

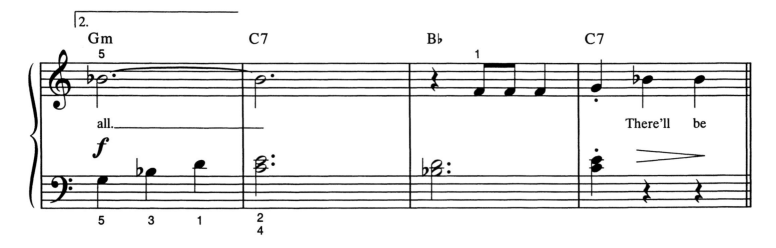

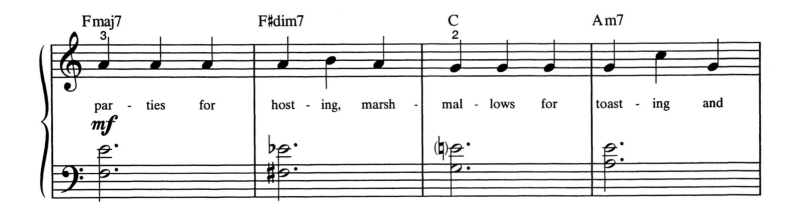

The Most Wonderful Time of Year - 3 - 2
AFM0406

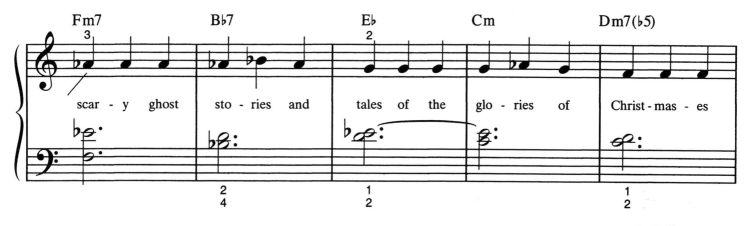

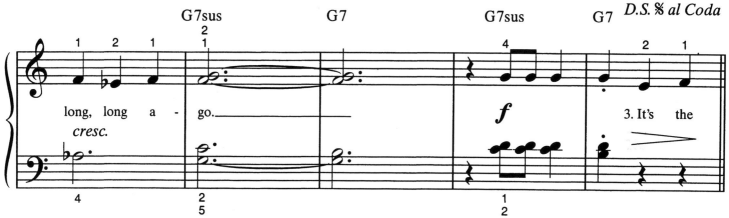

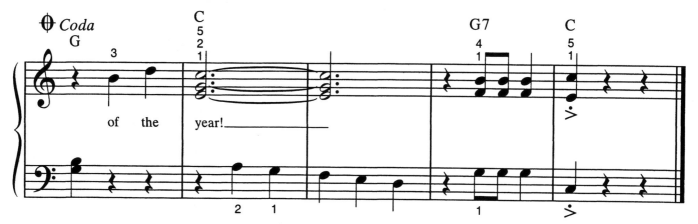

Verse 3:
It's the most wonderful time of the year.
There'll be much mistletoeing
And hearts will be glowing
When loved ones are near.
It's the most wonderful time of the year!

JINGLE BELLS

Music and Lyrics by
JAMES PIERPONT
Arranged by DAN COATES

Brightly

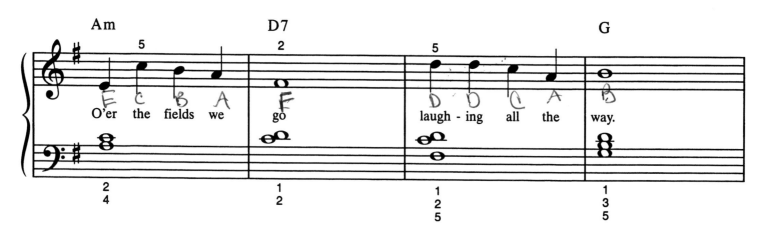

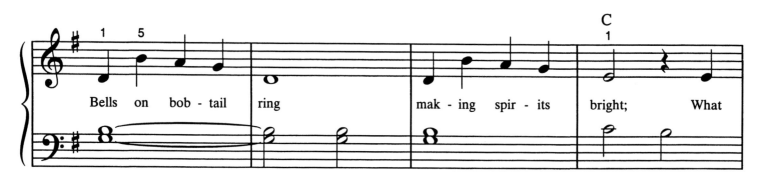

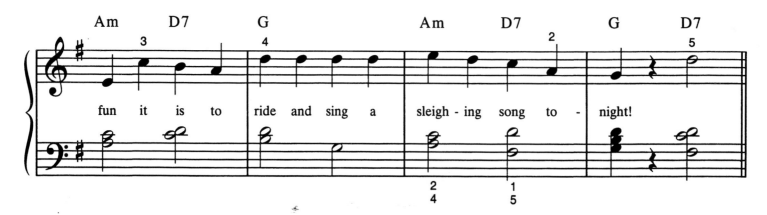

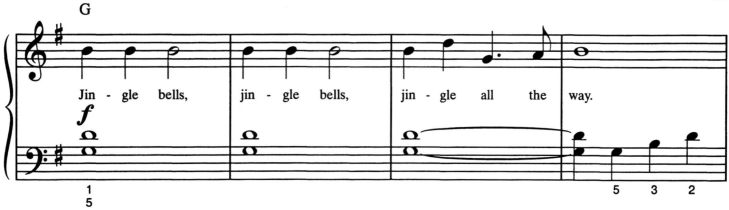

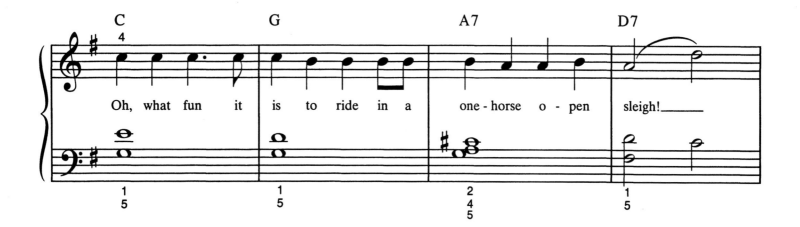

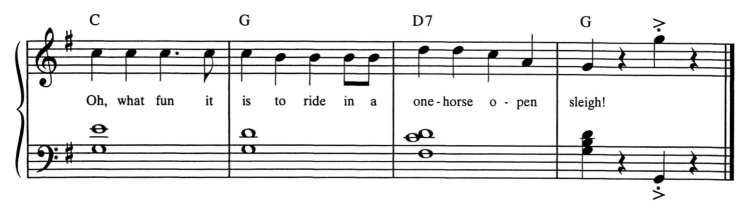

LET IT SNOW! LET IT SNOW! LET IT SNOW!

Lyric by
SAMMY CAHN

Music by
JULE STYNE
Arranged by DAN COATES

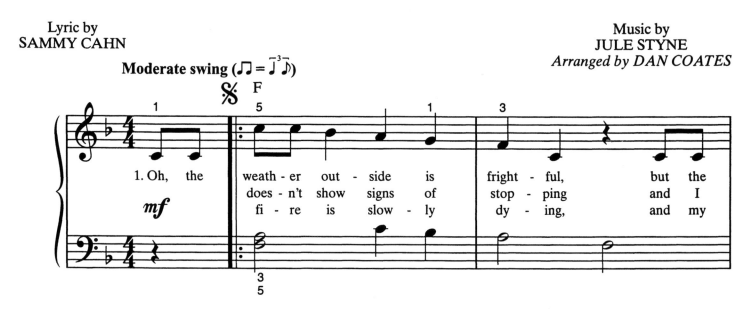

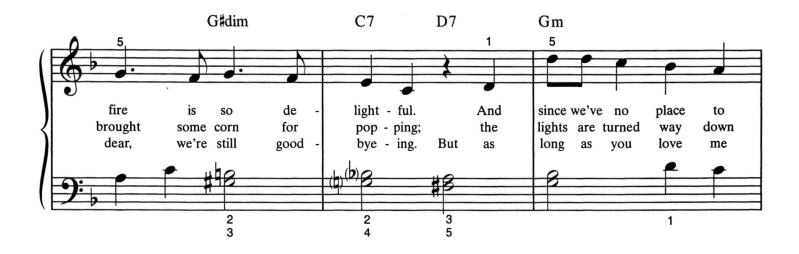

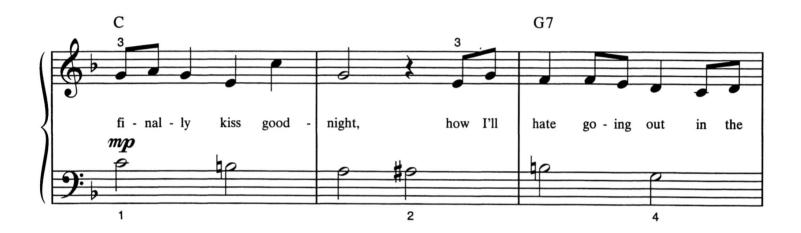

Let It Snow! Let It Snow! Let It Snow! - 2 - 2
AFM0406

SANTA CLAUS IS COMIN' TO TOWN

Words by
HAVEN GILLESPIE

Music by
J. FRED COOTS
Arranged by DAN COATES

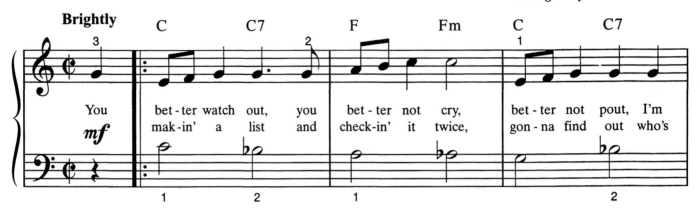

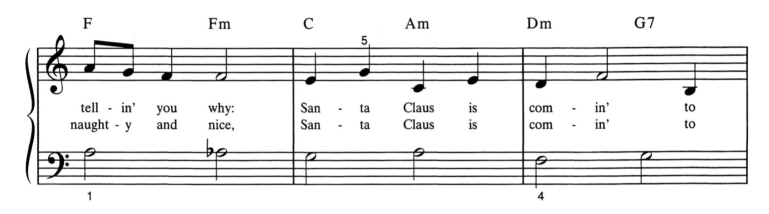

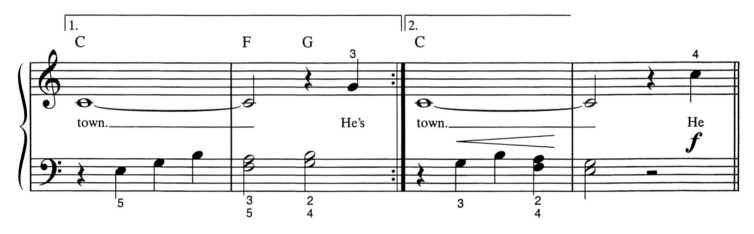

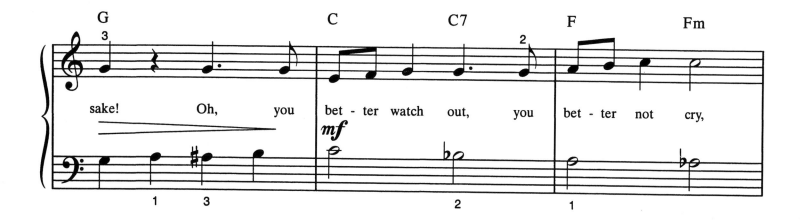

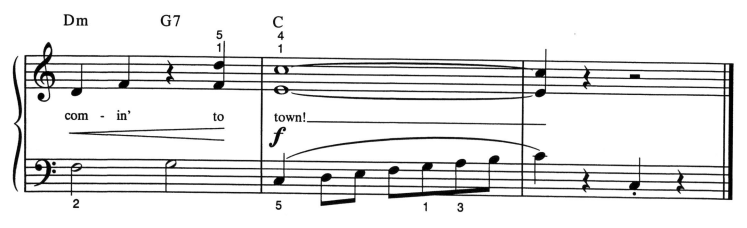

Santa Claus Is Comin' to Town - 2 - 2
AFM0406

SLEIGH RIDE

Words by
MITCHELL PARISH

Music by
LEROY ANDERSON
Arranged by DAN COATES

Bright, steady tempo

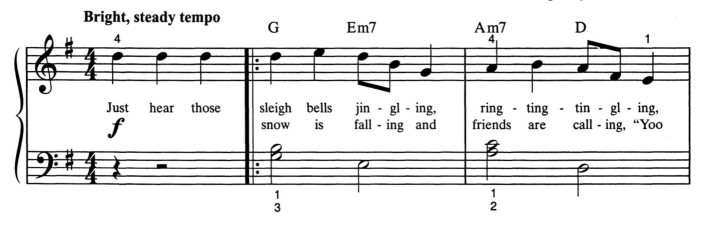

Just hear those sleigh bells jin - gl - ing, ring - ting - tin - gl - ing,
snow is fall - ing and friends are call - ing, "Yoo

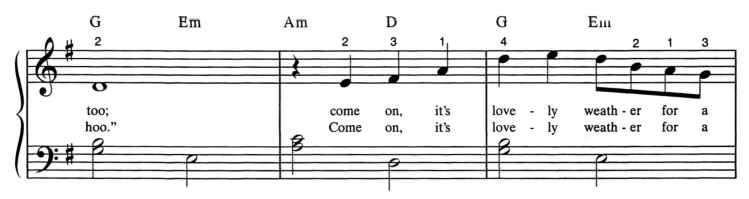

too; come on, it's love - ly weath - er for a
hoo." Come on, it's love - ly weath - er for a

sleigh ride to - geth - er with you.
sleigh ride to - geth - er with Out - side, the

you. *dim.* Gid - dy - yap, gid - dy - yap, gid - dy -

Sleigh Ride - 3 - 1
AFM0406

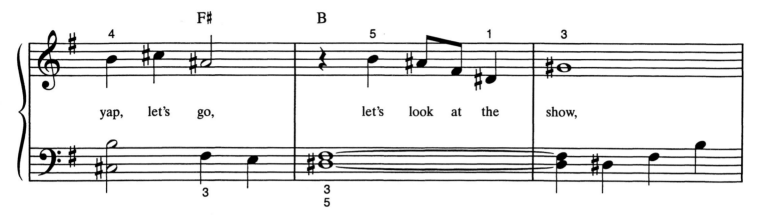

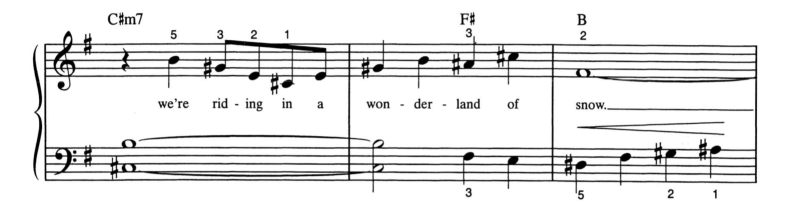

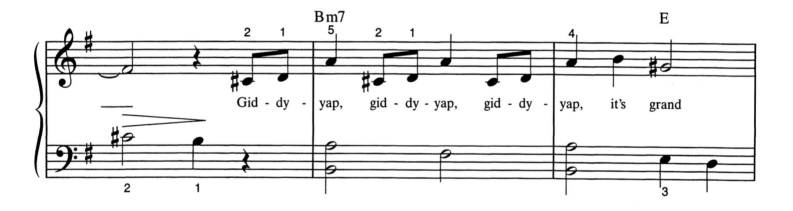

18

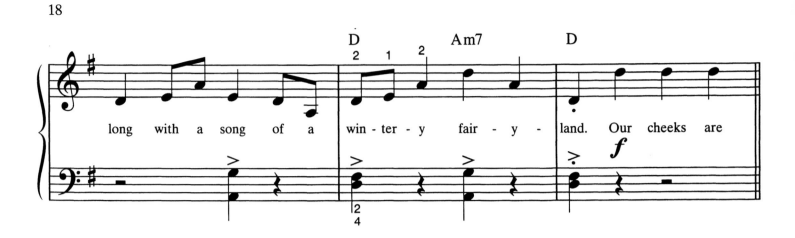

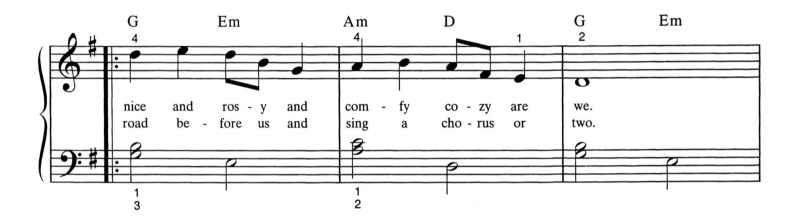

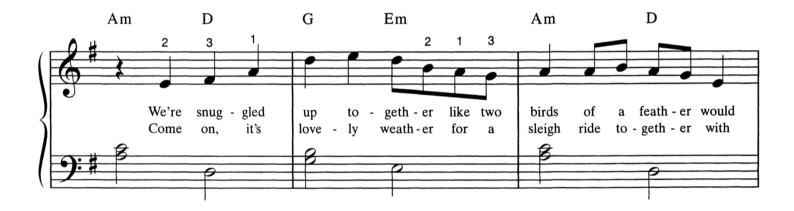

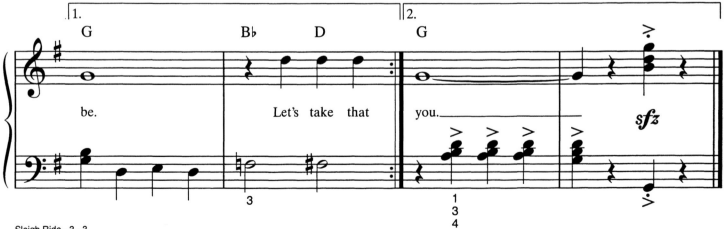

Sleigh Ride - 3 - 3
AFM0406

THE TWELVE DAYS OF CHRISTMAS

OLD ENGLISH
Arranged by DAN COATES

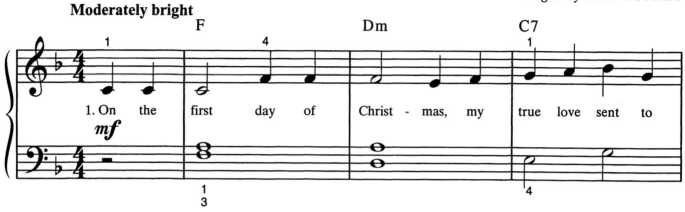

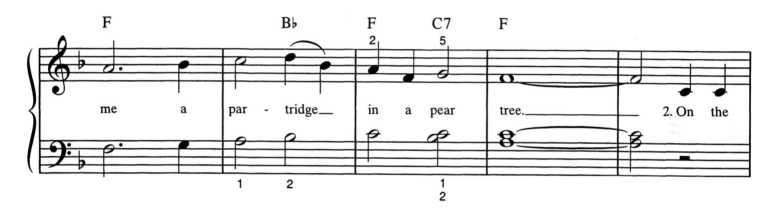

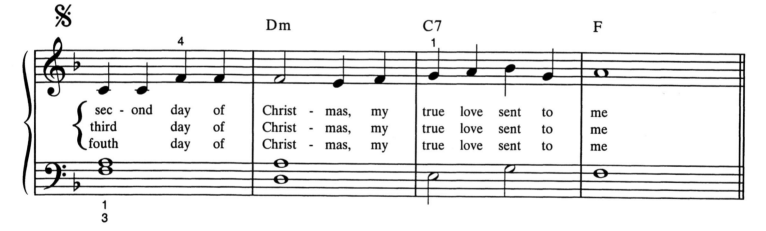

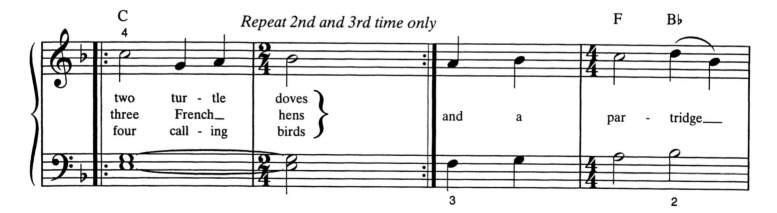

The Twelve Days of Christmas - 3 - 1
AFM0406

20

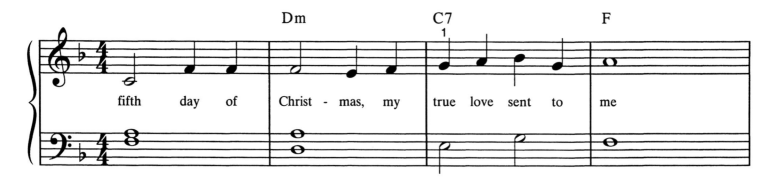

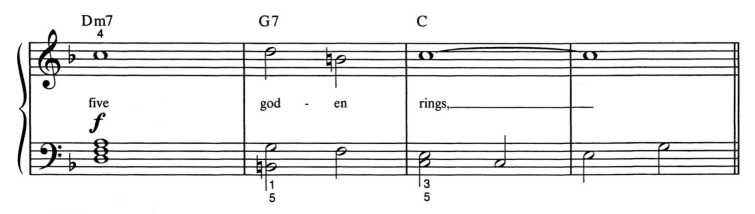

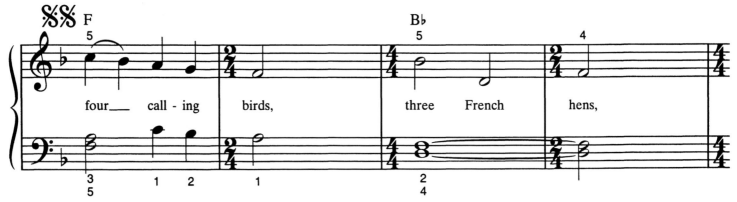

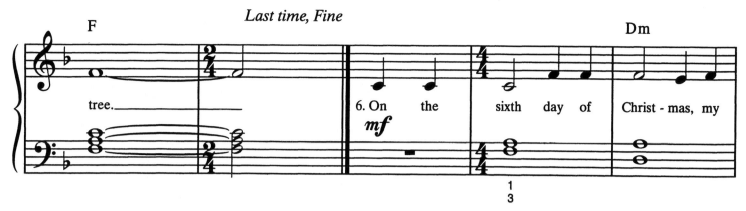

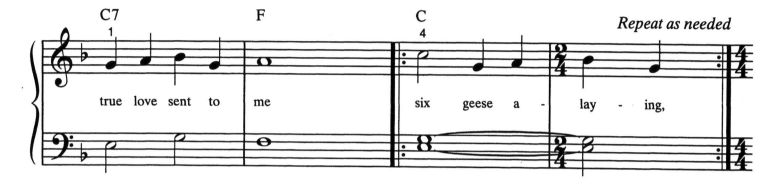

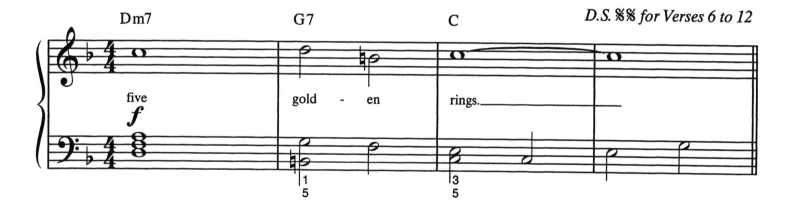

D.S. ℅℅ for Verses 6 to 12

7. On the seventh
8. On the eighth
9. On the ninth
10. On the tenth
11. On the eleventh
12. On the twelfth

day of Christmas, my true love sent to me

seven swans a-swimming,
eight maids a-milking,
nine ladies dancing,
ten lords a-leaping,
eleven pipers piping,
twelve drummers drumming,

five golden rings,

UP ON THE HOUSETOP

Music and Lyrics by
BENJAMIN RUSSELL HANBY
Arranged by DAN COATES

Brightly

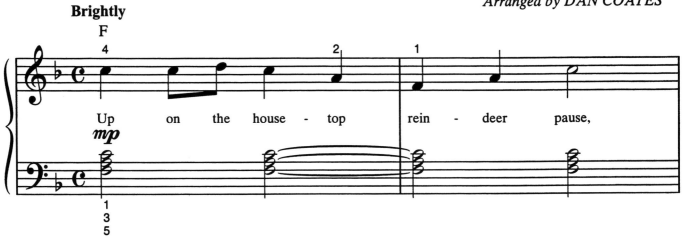

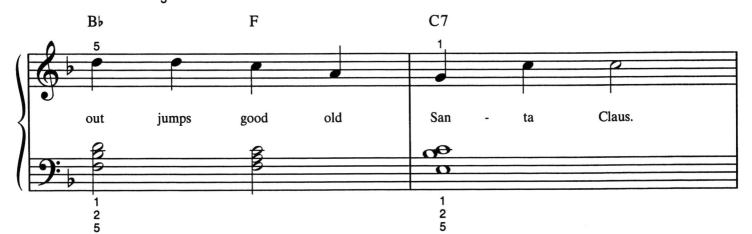

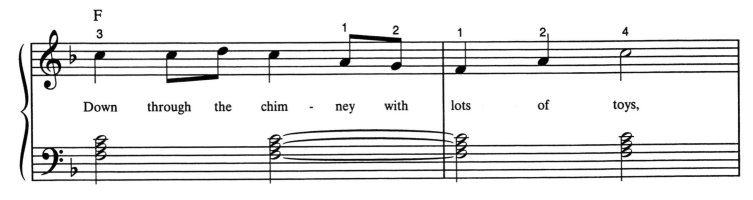

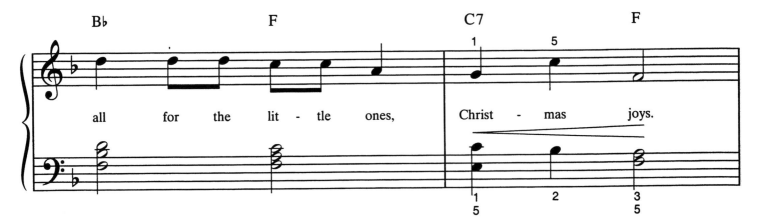

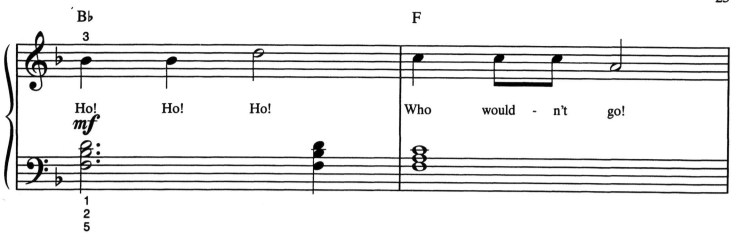

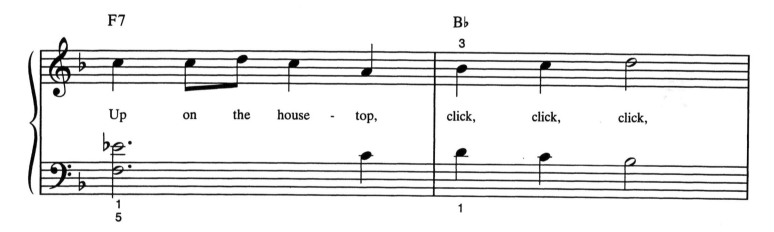

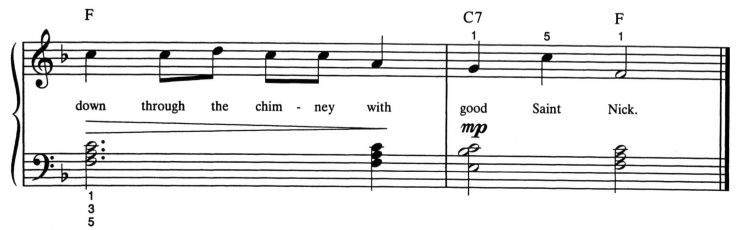

WE WISH YOU A MERRY CHRISTMAS

TRADITIONAL ENGLISH FOLK SONG
Arranged by DAN COATES

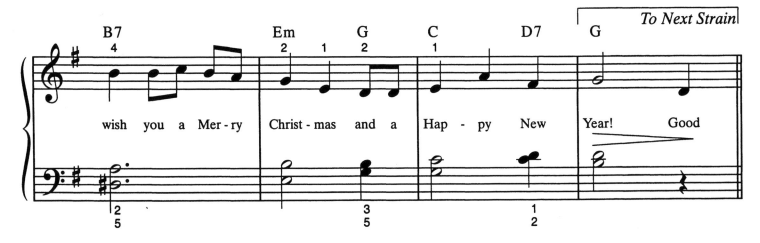

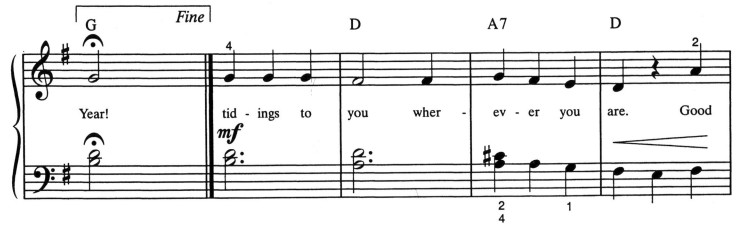